GW00725973

The Flesh Game

A Comedy for Women

Rae Shirley

Samuel French – London

New York – Sydney – Toronto – Hollywood

ESSEX COUNTY LIBRARY

FN55313

CHARACTERS

Carol
Judith
Nurse Burton
Rachel
Pauline
Jane
Sandra

The action takes place in the luxurious lounge of a modern Health Resort

Time—the present

During the play the Lights dim to denote a passage of time

_____

Dedicated to all would-be slimmers of whatever age, sex or creed in their efforts to fight the flab, and eschew the ever-present temptations of the flesh.

R.S.

PRODUCTION NOTE

Carol is getting married in a month's time, and wants to lose a stone. She is in her late twenties to early thirties. **Judith** is fortyish, a divorcee, slimming to help her in her search for pastures new. **Nurse Burton** is any age, but oldish if possible. **Rachel** is fortyish, an actress eager to get a part in a television play and trying to slim before her audition. **Pauline:** fiftyish, masculine type, very forthright and dominant. **Jane:** her younger sister, and "little Sir Echo". **Sandra:** any age between thirty and forty, a journalist.

If the actresses are slim, extra curves could be added by using padded underwear. There is the voice of a man, off stage, which could be played by a member of stage management

THE FLESH GAME*

The luxurious lounge of a modern Health Resort

It is morning

The lounge contains comfortable chairs, a couple of small tables and some books. There is an exit UL *which leads to the hall and other parts of the establishment*

As the CURTAIN *rises, Carol and Judith, each wearing a négligé, are sitting determinedly getting through their breakfast, i.e. a glass of tepid water with a slice of lemon floating on top*

Carol I weighed myself this morning, and I've lost one pound, two ounces.

Judith No kidding! What scales did you use?

Carol My bathroom one, of course.

Judith That's faulty. That's why Nurse Burton always uses the big one.

Carol You sure it's faulty?

Judith Something to do with it being on carpet. It's got to be on proper lino to register properly.

Carol I wish you hadn't told me. You weighed yourself today?

Judith Give us a chance. It's not 10 o'clock yet.

Carol The earlier, the better. I always seem to weigh more as the day goes on.

Judith (*holding up the lemon juice contemptuously*) On this diet!

Carol It's true, Judith. Something to do with the atmosphere.

Judith For crying out loud! What's the atmosphere got to do with your weight?

Carol I read it in a book. It definitely said the atmosphere affects your weight. I mean, look what happens to the men when they get to the moon—floating about like rubber dummies all over the place.

---

*NB. Paragraph 3 on page ii of this Acting Edition regarding photocopying and video-recording should be carefully read.

1

Judith That, my sweet, is the law of gravity.

Carol Law of gravity? Never heard of it.

Judith Don't ask me to explain. (*Sipping her drink*) God, this tastes foul! All I know is, it's the force which keeps your two feet on the ground.

Carol I could do with some of that when I'm with Peter.

Judith Sweeps you off your feet, does he?

Carol (*rapturously*) Does he! He's only got to look at me, and I'm on Cloud Nine.

Judith H'mmm ... you're obviously not married to him!

Carol But I'm going to be—four weeks next Saturday.

Judith Oh?

Carol The fact of the matter is (*confidentially*)—I've bought my wedding dress.

Judith Congratulations!

Carol Size 12, and I'm, well—I'm not size 12, am I?

Judith No, dear. You are not. I can see that without my glasses.

Carol And they wouldn't change it. So here I am. I've got to lose—well, as much as possible.

Judith Why on earth did you buy that size in the first place?

Carol I bought it 6 months ago, only Peter kept putting the wedding date off. Said he wanted promotion first. At the time it was too tight for me, but now! Now I look like a whale fighting to get out of a sardine skin.

Judith I know the feeling.

Carol And you know how persuasive some of those shop assistants can be. (*Affecting a South Kensington drawl*) Madam looks absolutely fantastic in that gown! It was positively made for madam! (*In her own voice*) So, like a fool, I fell for it.

Judith What does Peter say to all this?

Carol Oh, he doesn't know. I'm not that much of a fool.

Judith Where does he think you are now?

Carol I didn't dare tell him I was going to a Health Farm to reduce. So I said I was going on a special cookery course. You know, the genuine Cordon Bleu thing. So that I could make him some wonderful dishes after we're married.

Judith Well, you won't get many ideas here for wonderful dishes, and that's a fact.

Nurse Burton enters all breeze and bonhomie

Nurse Good morning, ladies! And how are we this morning?

Enjoying your lovely breakfast, I see. But where are the others? Surely they haven't finished already?

Judith So far as we know, they haven't even started.

Nurse Haven't even started! Tut, tut. We can't have this kind of thing, can we? Routine and Discipline. These are the Watchwords, the Order of the Day, in the Eldorado Health Farm, and must be maintained at all costs. I repeat, ladies, At All Costs. (*Going into an obviously oft repeated spiel*) We are here to encourage our bodies to ignore the Temptation of Food. Eating is the curse of our western civilization. We are what we eat. If we eat dead food, we are dead from the neck up.

Judith What about the rest of the body—from the neck down? Mine's started to complain bitterly. In fact, I had a rebellion on my hands last night after supper.

Nurse A rebellion on your hands? What do you mean?

Judith I threw up.

Nurse Threw up!

Carol She means she was sick. And so was I.

Judith It was the carrot juice and yoghurt cocktail after the bran mash soufflé that did it.

Nurse (*beaming*) Splendid, splendid! Now that is what I like to hear. It means your body is having a spring-clean, a genuine clearance sale. After years of insulting your bodies with duck and green peas, lamb and mint sauce, and all that rubbish—all Dead Food, don't forget!—now your body is telling you what is good for you.

Judith You could have fooled me! That's not the kind of message my body is getting.

Carol Same here. If it weren't for that wedding dress. . . .

Nurse Don't you see you are giving your poor overworked bodies a complete rest? You must listen to your bodies. Listen, and do what they tell you.

Judith Even when it tells you to be sick!

Nurse (*rapturously*) Above all, when it tells you to be sick!

Rachel enters dresed in a kaftan. She totters in and collapses into a chair, groaning

(*Brightly*) Good morning, Rachel. Have you had your breakfast?

Rachel (*looking at her vaguely*) Who—who are you?

Nurse You know perfectly well who I am, Rachel. I'm Nurse

Burton. I know you're an actress, dear, but we don't want any display of temperament, do we?

Rachel Temperament—with my stomach! Tell me, why am I paying good money for this week of torture. Go on, tell me, tell me.

Nurse Now, now, Rachel. We must not become hysterical. I repeat. Have you had your breakfast?

Rachel (*hollow-voiced*) Breakfast?

Nurse Your lovely glass of lemon water.

Rachel No, I have not had my lovely glass of lemon water. And if I weren't a lady, I'd tell you what to do with it.

Nurse I think she's a little distraught this morning.

Judith She's definitely a little something.

Rachel Shall I tell you what I'd like for breakfast? You won't say yes, but I'll tell you just the same. (*Sitting up, her eyes alight*) I'd like—I'd like—two, no, three rashers of bacon, cooked crisp as crisp. Scrambled eggs, two sausages, and a couple of kidneys for luck. Oh, and two rounds of fried bread. How's that for starters!

Nurse I thought she was hysterical. Now I do believe she's suffering from hallucinations.

Judith You're right. It would be hallucinating to see all that here. Like cool, rippling water in a desert.

Nurse I'm going to get the poor girl a nice glass of lemon water.

Nurse Burton exits

Rachel My head feels like a steel furnace going full blast and my stomach wants to know if my mouth's gone on strike. If only I'd known what it was going to be like, I'd never have come here.

Judith Why did you come here?

Rachel I'm auditioning for a part in a new play on telly. She's supposed to be slim and sylph-like ... you know, like we all were at sweet seventeen. My downfall is chocolate. No damn will power. I've only got to look at a bar of Mars at a checkout, and my knees go to water. So—I thought if I came here for a week ...

Judith Have you lost any weight?

Rachel Two pounds! Two miserable pounds. After hours in the heat treatment room, three mile walk every day, massaged till my bones cry out for mercy, sauna, aerobics, swimming ... you name it, I've had it. They keep telling me to listen to my body. I can't help listening to it. Get the hell out of here, it keeps saying! (*Sighing*) If it weren't for that part on telly . . .

Nurse Burton enters, carrying a glass of lemon water on a tray

Nurse Here we are, dear. Your breakfast. I managed to persuade Cook to give you an extra slice of lemon.

Rachel takes the glass in silence

Drink it up like a good girl.

Rachel takes a sip, shudders, slams down the glass on the nearest table, and makes a frenzied exit, hand to mouth

Well, really! There's gratitude for you!

Judith And after Cook being so kind—that extra slice of lemon!

Nurse Do I detect a note of sarcasm, Judith?

Judith What—me? Not at all, Nurse. Pure jealousy, that's all. We've never had an extra slice of lemon, have we, Carol?

Carol Never!

Nurse (*graciously*) Well, if you're good . . . Cook can be rather awkward at times, but I'll see what I can do.

Judith (*overdoing it*) Oh, thank you, Nurse. I know we can rely on you.

Nurse Have you seen the sisters this morning?

Carol Only heard them.

Nurse Heard them? What do you mean?

Carol My bedroom's next door to theirs, and they were having a duet.

Nurse A duet? Really! I didn't know they could sing.

Carol They can't. They were snoring.

Nurse How extraordinary! Not many of our ladies snore. Our gentlemen, yes, but not the ladies.

Carol I've often wondered about one of them. The sisters, I mean.

Judith What d'you mean—wondered?

Carol Well, the big one is so terribly masculine, isn't she? That moustache . . .

Nurse I do think you're being rather catty, dear. A few faint hairs on the upper lip is common to many of our sex.

Judith Not that faint, Nurse.

Carol And she shaves, you know—and I don't mean her legs.

Nurse How do you know?

Carol I went into her room by mistake yesterday, and she was lathering her chin like a sailor home on leave.

Nurse Probably trying out a new face cream.

Carol I doubt it. She removed it with a cut-throat razor.

Nurse A cut-throat razor! Are you sure, Carol?

Carol Well, I wasn't wearing my contact lenses, but it certainly looked like it. And when she—or is it he?—cut herself, the language all but straightened my perm.

Pauline and Jane enter. Pauline, as usual leading the way, Jane her dutiful follower, bringing up the rear. Pauline seems to be thriving on the restricted health farm diet. She is dressed in masculine type trouser suit, heavy shoes, etc.

Pauline (*booming*) Good morning, everybody. I hope you all slept well. Don't hover, Jane. Go and sit down.

Jane Yes, Pauline, dear.

Nurse Have you had your breakfast, ladies?

Pauline Of course, Nurse. Hours ago.

Jane Hours ago.

Pauline The lemon juice seemed even more lemony than usual. Delicious!

Jane Delicious!

Nurse I'm delighted to have at least two satisfied customers. I must be off. (*Turning at the exit*) Cook tells me we are having a little extra something for lunch. Something special.

Judith Great! What is it?

Nurse (*pretending to hesitate*) I shouldn't really, but ...

Carol Come on, Nurse. Be a sport!

Nurse Promise you'll pretend it's a lovely surprise.

Carol We promise.

Nurse It's bran soup, with a dash of yoghurt.

Nurse Burton exits

Carol (*groaning*) Bran soup with a dash of yoghurt! I can't wait!

Judith Well, take your choice. It's either that or another glass of lemon water.

Pauline Jane and I are off down to the village. Any of you lot feel like coming?

Carol I can't. It's my day for aerobics and heat treatment.

Pauline It's my day, too, but I'm giving it a miss.

Judith You're forever trotting down to the village. What's the attraction?

Pauline What do you think it is! Food, of course, lovely, lovely food.

Jane Food, of course. Lovely, lovely food.

Carol Good Lord! You mean to say you go down to the village to eat?

Pauline Like a horse.

Jane Like two horses!

Pauline Jane! Don't exaggerate!

Judith My God! Now I've heard everything!

Pauline Best fish and chips this side of London.

Jane Best fish and chips this side of London.

Judith But, Pauline, if they ever found out . . .?

Pauline Let 'em! My first day here, after pushing down that All Bran soufflé, I said — That's all right for starters. What's the next course?

Carol You didn't!

Pauline I damn well did. They made me feel like Oliver Twist. So I said to myself — sod this for a lark! I'm off for a pub meal the first chance I get.

Judith But what about losing weight? That's what you're here for . . . (*doubtfully*) . . . isn't it?

Pauline Losing weight nothing. I'm here for a bet. Two hundred quid if I stick it for a week. The diet wasn't mentioned.

Judith Whoever made that bet with you must have been a fool.

Pauline You're right. It was my husband.

Jane Her husband.

Judith I didn't know you were married.

Pauline Oh, yes. More or less.

Judith What does that mean?

Pauline The longer we're married, the less it means.

Judith Sounds familiar.

Pauline You know. First separate beds, then separate rooms. Now it's separate homes. The way we're going on, soon it will be separate countries.

Carol I'd hate that.

Pauline You married?

Carol Not yet.

Pauline I'll talk to you in a couple of years' time.

Judith It must get a bit pricey. Separate houses, all that.

Pauline Oh, he's loaded. He's an oil tycoon.

Carol You mean he's an Arab?

Pauline Rich enough to be one. Bought oil shares when they were rock bottom, and now the lolly's like the oil—pouring in.

Jane Pouring in.

Judith You married, Jane?

Jane (*shyly*) Oh, no. I'm not married. I'm—er—er—you know—a bit—er—er—you know.

Judith No. I don't know.

Pauline She thinks men are God's gift to the universe. Practically bends the knee every time she sees one. Sticks them on a pedestal as high as the Eiffel Tower.

Judith Couldn't you have enlightened her?

Pauline Enlightened her? I've all but drawn diagrams trying to show what a rotten lot they are, but no good. She can be stubborn, you know. Dead stubborn. Keeps me awake at night sometimes.

Jane (*rapturously*) Keeps me awake at nights, too!

Pauline See what I mean? You've only got to breathe the word man, and she goes berserk. Jane, stop making a fool of yourself.

Sandra enters, attractively dressed

Sandra Hi, everybody! How's things?

Judith You're nauseatingly cheerful this morning. Does that mean you haven't had your breakfast?

Sandra Breakfast! What breakfast?

Judith Only one breakfast in this establishment as far as I know. That Cordon Bleu glass of tepid lemon water.

Sandra You've got to be kidding! I've chucked it down the loo every morning since I've been here.

Pauline Then how come you've supposed to have lost over a stone in a week?

Sandra A-a-ah! That would be telling wouldn't it!

Carol I don't believe you have lost it.

Sandra Believe what you like! I'm not here to lose weight, anyway.

Judith What are you here for, then?

Sandra I'm an investigative journalist. I'm writing a book on Health Farms.

Judith Are you now? Do the powers-that-be know this?

Sandra Don't be ridiculous! I shouldn't have mentioned it now, so for goodness sake, keep it under your hat, all of you.

Judith Okay. So long as you tell us how you've managed to lose weight. You certainly look as if you have.

Sandra Elementary, my dear Watson! I sewed some tiny bags of sand inside my panties at the first weigh-in, and have been discarding them one at a time ever since.

Pauline Wished I'd thought of that. Clever. Damn clever.

Jane Clever. Damn clever.

Pauline Jane! Watch your language!

Judith This book you're going to write—are you giving the absolute low-down?

Sandra I'll say! All I'm hoping is that they'll try and stop publication, then I'll be laughing all the way to the bank.

Pauline How come?

Sandra The publicity, Pauline, the publicity! People will probably think it's pornographic, and I'll be made!

Judith Why didn't I think of it!

Sandra And tonight's my last night. The graduation dinner.

Judith Lucky devil!

Sandra Roast pork, apple sauce, roast potatoes, veg, assorted wines!

Judith Stop it, stop it!

Sandra And men galore!

Jane (*rapturously*) Men galore!

Pauline She's off again!

Sandra Always a wild night, the last night. This is the fourth Health Farm I've been to in the last three months, and the final night gets better and better.

Judith Well, go on! Tell us! What does happen?

Sandra Everything, love, everything! One Health Farm I went to had a foolproof system of counting calories. You lose so many swimming, so many walking, etc., etc. One number I'll never forget, nor what it was for.

Carol What number?

Sandra Two hundred.

Judith Well, go on. What was it for?

Sandra For a spot of How's-your-father! One guy stuck a notice up on the board: "Anybody wanting to join me burning up 200 calories—Room nineteen, any time after eight."

Judith I can't see any of the beauties we've got here lashing out.
Sandra That's just it, Judith. You never know! The last night most of them cast off their lamb's clothing, and out come the wolves. And there's that Dickie Steele. He's an absolute darling.
Carol Did it work—that guy putting up that notice?
Sandra Must have. He lost pounds, and looked absolutely knackered the rest of the week.
Pauline (*grinning*) This is no place for a parson's daughter! I'm off to the village for some grub. Come along, Jane. Anybody else coming?
Sandra Not this morning. Later, perhaps.

Pauline and Jane exit

Judith You're on that fish and chip bender, too, are you?
Sandra Here I am, though I have stuck the whole diet thing out for a whole week in one Health Farm I went to. Nearly killed me, it did. Never again. Had to see it through for the sake of my book.
Judith It's nearly killing Rachel. The poor thing's got the lemon d.t's.
Carol We all know that feeling. Well, I'm off for my happy hour in the Heat Room.
Judith And I'm for my aerobics and massage.
Sandra And the best of British luck!
Judith Thanks. I know we'll need it.

Judith and Carol exit

Sandra takes out a notebook and pen from her voluminous handbag, and starts to write

Nurse Burton enters

Sandra hastily returns her notebook to her bag

Nurse Ah, good morning, Sandra. Have you had your breakfast?
Sandra (*sweetly*) Of course, nurse. I actually requested an extra glass.
Nurse Good girl. I wish all our ladies were as appreciative as you. Your weight loss has been so encouraging. An excellent testimonial to our Health Farm. As the Principal said to me only last night—Sandra is our star patient. She has taken our doctrine to heart, and is aware of the hazards of eating, the poison we inject

into our defenceless bodies by consuming dead food. You know
we have an Honours system here in which our best client is
presented with a medal after the graduation dinner.

Sandra (*vastly interested*) Really! This is most interesting.

Nurse And, just between you and me, dear, a little bird has
whispered that you are well in the running for this important
award.

Sandra Oh, Nurse! I am quite overwhelmed! I really am!

Nurse We call it the Mini-Meal Olympic Medal.

Sandra The Mini-Meal Olympic Medal! And I've won it!

Nurse Ssh! Not a word to a soul, dear. This is just between
ourselves. Mr Richard Steele was a prime favourite until
recently, but, alas, he has fallen by the wayside.

Sandra Dickie Steele? Er—how did he fall?

Nurse I am sorry to say that the last two nights he has come to
dinner smelling strongly of beer.

Sandra (*apparently shocked*) How awful! And his last night
tonight.

Nurse Yes. We do find that with some of our gentlemen they seem
to falter by the end of the week. Sad, very sad.

Sandra Ah, well, we must make allowances. After all, they're only
human.

Nurse True, true, but some are definitely more human than
others. The trouble is, they stop listening to their bodies.

Sandra Perhaps by the end of the week they've become a little
deaf.

Nurse Surely not. A little shaky about the knees, perhaps. It does
affect some of them in that way. And sometimes they start
wandering about after lights-out . . . they seem to have lost their
way to the bedroom. Most mysterious. Well, I must get on with
my work. And don't forget, dear. Not a word.

Sandra Not a word?

Nurse About your Mini-Meal Olympic Medal.

Sandra Oh, that! Oh, no! Not a word.

Nurse Burton exits

*Sandra again takes out her notebook, and tries to settle down to
some more writing*

Rachel enters, brandishing the Daily Mail, *obviously very upset*

Rachel Have you seen this? Have you? After all I've been through! Have you seen it?
Sandra Pipe down, love. Seen what?
Rachel Read it, read it!

Rachel thrusts the paper at Sandra, then exits in a storm of sobs

Sandra looks after Rachel in some concern, scans the paper, turning over the pages

Sandra Nothing to get excited about here. America accuses Russia of deception over arms race. Russia accuses America of spying. So what's new! Another bomb scare in the West End. I know the poor dear is an actress and they're always temperamental, but if every one threw a fit every time they read the paper ... Better go and see if I can do something to help.

Sandra exits

The Lights dim momentarily to denote a passage of time. It is now evening of the same day, and we can hear sounds of revelry from off stage. Dance music, perhaps some rather uncertain masculine voices trying to sing

Pauline (*off; loudly*) Have you seen Jane?
Man's voice (*off, in a voice slurred with drink*) Jane? Jane—who?
Pauline (*off*) Never mind!

Pauline enters, now in an evening trouser suit. As she enters, she calls out

Jane! Jane!

Nurse Burton enters

Nurse Were you calling, Pauline?
Pauline What did it sound like? Of course I was calling. I've lost Jane.
Nurse Lost Jane? How on earth could anybody lose anyone here? She's bound to be in the building.
Pauline There are thirty-five bedrooms, Nurse, and nineteen bathrooms. She could be in any of them.
Nurse (*primly*) Not in *any* of the bedrooms, surely. Not Jane!
Pauline If she's lost, God knows where she could be. (*Inspired*) I

know! I'll ask the Principal to make an announcement. Has anybody seen Jane?

Nurse Don't be ridiculous, Pauline. This is her busy night—the graduation dinner and all the work that entails. You know, you're apt to fuss far too much over that sister of yours. I'm quite sure she's quite capable of looking after herself. Why don't you go back to your room and see if she's there.

Pauline I've already looked there. Three times.

Nurse What about the bathrooms? Have you looked in them?

Pauline I have. All nineteen of them.

Nurse She may be in the grounds. It's a lovely moonlit night.

Pauline She won't be there. She's afraid of the dark.

Nurse Now, I must attend to my duties. As I've already said, Pauline, I think you fuss far too much.

Nurse Burton exits

Pauline (*angrily*) Fuss too much! Silly old sod!

Sandra enters, looking very glamorous in evening dress. She has a glass of wine in her hand and around her neck she wears a medallion on a chain. This is, of course, the Mini-Meal Olympic Medal

Have you seen Jane, Sandra?

Sandra Let me think ... yes?

Pauline Where?

Sandra In the bar.

Pauline (*horrified*) In the bar! Jane?

Sandra (*sitting, and sipping her wine*) For goodness sake, she's not under age, is she!

Pauline Was she—was she on her own?

Sandra Don't be silly! Nobody's on their own in a bar!

Pauline Sandra! Who was she with?

Sandra (*enjoying herself*) Who d'you think! A man, of course.

Pauline A man? Are you sure?

Sandra Pauline dear, I know a man when I see one!

Pauline Who was he? What was his name?

Sandra Don't know his name, but he'd more than a couple to drink.

Pauline (*horrified*) You mean he was drunk?

Sandra Well, he wasn't sober.

Pauline Oh, my God! I must find her, I must find her!

Pauline exits in a frenzied rush

Sandra (*looking after her, thoughtfully*) Can't help wondering about her sometimes

Rachel enters in evening dress, more composed now, but she looks as if she's been crying

So there you are! Where've you been all day?

Rachel (*defiantly*) What's it to you!

Sandra All right, all right! No need to be so damn aggressive. I thought if you needed a shoulder to cry on— (*indicating her own shoulder*)—here's one on offer.

Rachel I'm quite capable of crying without the help of your shoulder or anyone else's.

Sandra Okay, love, okay. Stay up there on your high horse, but high horses can get pretty lonely, you know—stuck up there in that rarefied atmosphere.

Rachel You can stop trying to be clever and literary. I am not impressed.

Sandra Let's start again, shall we? You came rushing in here this morning looking like Lady Macbeth when she's just seen the blood on her hands. You hurl today's paper at me—then stampede out, still doing your tragedy queen act—and that was the last I've seen of you all day. I've hammered on your door—I knew you were in—but Answer Came There None!

Rachel I gave you the paper, didn't I? Didn't you read it?

Sandra I read it, but didn't see anything there to cause such a crisis. Only the usual crap. America accuses Russia. Russia accuses America. So what's new?

Rachel Oh, shut up, Sandra! You read the wrong page. It was that Miriam Golding. She's got the part on telly I was after. It was in Nigel Dempster's gossip column. You must have seen it.

Sandra Well, I didn't. For the simple reason I never read him. He's been proved wrong before, you know.

Rachel (*sighing*) Not this time, Sandra. I knew she was in the running, but I just kept on hoping. I *had* to keep on hoping, didn't I?

Sandra Oh, yes. We've all of us always got to keep on hoping. Miriam Golding ... I'm sorry, Rachel, truly I am.

Rachel If only she couldn't act I wouldn't say anything. Now I'm being bitchy. She can act. And of course she's younger than I am. (*With a wry smile*) They all seem to be getting younger these days ... all except me.

Sandra There'll be other parts, Rachel ... bound to be other parts.

Rachel D'you reckon? Oh, God, I hope so ... I hope so. Do you know how long it is since I had a decent part with more than three lines? Nearly two years. Two bloody years! I borrowed the money to come here. I've tried and tried. (*She laughs shakily*) I've had everything but a face-lift. And if I'd had the cash, I'd have had that!

Sandra I know what a jungle the theatre is. Biggest unemployment ratio in the country.

Rachel You don't have to tell me. I'm one of them.

Sandra You ever thought of doing something else?

Rachel Thought of it! You name it, I've done it. Barmaid, waitress, window cleaner. I had to give that up. Kept falling off the ladder.

Sandra Can you type?

Rachel Only two fingers, but I can work up to a fair speed. I can spell, too!

Sandra Our office could do with another typist. Feel like having a bash?

Rachel Are you serious?

Sandra If I weren't, I wouldn't have mentioned it.

Rachel (*excitedly hugging her*) You're on! When do I start?

Sandra End of the week, when we've finished our hard labour here.

Rachel I'm not putting up with this till the end of the week. No more of that poisonous lemon water, no more listening to my body. Now it will have to listen to me for a change. Oh, Sandra, darling, you've saved my life.

Sandra And if you feel up to doing some overtime, you can start typing my book for me.

Rachel Marvellous! Oh, Sandra, I could hug you!

Sandra You just this minute have, dear!

Rachel Your book, you said. What book?

Sandra The book I'm writing. "The Flesh Game".

Rachel "The Flesh Game"? Smashing title. Is it pornographic?

Sandra Some people may think so. Actually, it's the lowdown on Health Farms.

Rachel No kidding! The lowdown, eh? That's great! Maybe I could supply you with some juicy details.

Sandra All gratefully accepted and acknowledged. Feel like a drink to celebrate?

Rachel So long as it isn't tepid lemon water!

Judith and Carol enter in attractive evening dress. Each is carrying a bottle and a glass, but these are concealed behind them

Sandra We were just going for a drink. Care to join us?

Judith There's a mob six feet deep around the bar—

Carol —but we've got reinforcements!

With a flourish, they produce their bottles and glasses

Rachel Manna in Egypt!

Carol But we've only got two glasses.

Sandra Three. I've got one.

Judith I'm not fussy. I've drunk out of a bottle before! Come on, Carol. Let's do the honours.

They start pouring out the wine

Carol Careful, Judith, or you'll spill it.

The glasses are handed out

Sandra We must all drink a toast.

Everyone stands

Rachel I know! To—duck and green peas!

Judith To—roast pork and apple sauce!

Sandra To—lamb and mint sauce!

Carol To—fish and chips for ever!

Laughing, they all drink, start coughing and spluttering

Sandra (*regarding drink sceptically*) Good God! What is it?

Judith Haven't a clue. Got it in the village pub. The landlord didn't know either.

Carol All he did know was it had been there since the last war. He thinks the Americans left it behind.

Sandra I'm not surprised! It's got a kick like a mule. You two are a bit tight already, aren't you?

Carol Not to worry. We've lined our stomachs with a good foundation. Had a good meal before we started.

Rachel A good meal? Where?

Carol In the pub, where d'you think. Piping hot pies, and chips from the chippy next door. Heaven, pure heaven!

Judith Which reminds me, have you seen the notice board?

Sandra Not today I haven't.

Rachel Neither have I.

Judith (*all smiles*) We have, haven't we, Carol?

Carol (*grinning*) I'll say we have!

Sandra So?

Judith Some joker's gone and put up that two hundred calorie notice.

Sandra No!

Judith Yes!

Sandra What room number did he give?

Judith Number ten.

Rachel I'm not with you. What's all this about?

Sandra It's a question of counting the calories, and how to lose them. Painlessly!

Rachel Well?

Sandra So many for swimming, so many for walking, etc., etc. And for a spot of You-Know-What—bang goes another two hundred!

Rachel And you mean to say that some guy has stuck that up on the board!

Sandra Got it in one! Room ten, did you say?

Judith That's right!

Sandra That's Dickie Steele's room. There'll be a queue outside his door a mile long!

Pauline enters

Pauline Has anyone here seen Jane?

They all shake their heads, trying not to laugh

Judith Have you looked in all the bedrooms?

Pauline Nurse Burton asked me that. Of course I have. All except number ten, that is.

They start to giggle, looking at each other

Sandra Why not number ten?

Pauline There was a notice on the door. "Do Not Disturb. Suffering from Migraine". So obviously I couldn't go in. What the hell are you all laughing at?

Judith S-sorry, Pauline . . . we . . . we had a joke . . . just before you came in. It's—it's—er– sort-of funny.

Pauline Well? What is the joke?

Sandra You—you're too young, Pauline.

Pauline You're drunk, the lot of you.

Sandra (*trying to be serious*) Pauline, how can you say such a thing! Have a drink.

Pauline I don't want your rotten drink!

Judith Of course you do. You're not here to lose weight. You told us. Come on!

Pauline We-el . . . if you give my arm a jolly good twist.

Sandra Glass, somebody, glass!

Carol (*hastily wipes hers, and refills it*) One minute! Here we are, Pauline. A drop of the genuine stuff.

Pauline Genuine stuff? What is it?

Carol A-ah! There you have me. Don't remember exactly, but it is the genuine stuff. The man said.

Pauline Man? What man?

Judith The man in the pub, of course. The landlord.

Pauline Oh, he's okay. I've had some good drinks with him. (*She drinks, and then shudders*) My God! What is this? Bootleg alcohol!

Sandra Genuine stuff, Pauline. The real McCoy!

Pauline takes another swallow

Pauline It's the real something. You know, once you've got the first lot down you, it really isn't so bad.

Judith Good. Drink up and have another. We'll all have another.

Pauline (*peering at the medallion around Sandra's neck*) What's that you've got there, Sandra?

Sandra Thank you, Pauline. You're the first one to notice it. In case you girls don't happen to know, I am the Star Candidate for the week—so—I have been presented with Mini-Meal Olympic Medal! What d'you think of that!

Laughter from all of them, with a chorus of: You cheat! You of all people. If Nurse only knew! etc., etc.

(*Raising her hand to quell them*) I know, I know! I feel an awful fraud, but what could I do! When Nurse told me, I all but fell off my chair.

Judith Wait till they read your book!

Pauline Well, if it's any comfort to you, no-one else here deserves it either.

Jane enters. She looks ravishing

Pauline Jane! Where on earth have you been? I've been looking for you everywhere.

Jane (*sweetly*) I haven't really been anywhere, Pauline dear. I've only been counting calories!

CURTAIN

FURNITURE AND PROPERTY LIST

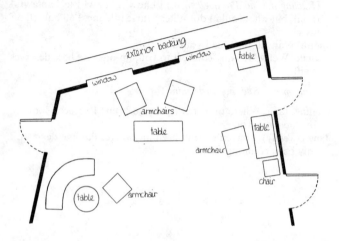

On stage: Two or three small tables. *On them:* books and magazines, two
glasses of lemon juice
Comfortable chairs
Dressing as desired

Off stage: Glass of lemon water **(Nurse)**
Daily Mail newspaper **(Rachel)**
Glass of wine **(Sandra)**
A bottle and a glass **(Judith)**
A bottle and a glass **(Carol)**

Personal: **Sandra:** voluminous handbag. *In it:* notebook and pen.
Medallion on a chain.

LIGHTING PLOT

Interior. The same scene throughout

To open: General lighting

Cue 1	**Sandra** exits *Dim lights to denote passage of time*	(Page 12)
Cue 2	Dance music is heard *Bring up lights to full*	(Page 12)

EFFECTS PLOT

Cue 1   After lights have dimmed   (Page 12)
           Sounds of revelry off, including dance music and male
           voices trying to sing

MADE AND PRINTED IN GREAT BRITAIN BY
LATIMER TREND & COMPANY LTD, PLYMOUTH
MADE IN ENGLAND